Dear Liz –
With hopes all
your dreams come true –

be well
Frances,

OVERFLOW

POEMS BY

HOPE TAYLOR-McGRIFF

BRYANT and DILLON PUBLISHERS, INC.
ORANGE, NEW JERSEY

Requests for permission to make copies of any part of the work should be mailed to: Permissions Department, Bryant and Dillon Publishers,Inc P.O. Box 39, Orange, New Jersey 07050

Library of Congress Cataloging in Publication Data
Taylor-McGriff, Hope, 1955-
Overflow.
(A Bryant and Dillon Book)
CIP # 93-72710
ISBN 0-9638672-0-2

Printed in the United States of America
10 9 8 7 6 5 4 3 2 1

To...

*the women of the "Gathering" who moved me to
put pen to paper.*

*Johanna and Andrea who listened to my work in
progress' whenever I called - even at 2, 3 or 4 a.m.*

*all the friends, colleagues and family members
who always "knew" this would happen.*

*the woman who inspired me to be - I am, forever,
your daughter.*

To all of you I dedicate this

OVERFLOW

CONTENTS

OVERFLOWING

OVERFLOWING

IN ANOTHER TIME

In another time, not so long ago,
the bracelets I wear
would have been chains that bound.

Learning to read
and openly praising my God
would have been punishable
by death.

In another time, not so long ago,
the physical pleasantness of my appearance
would have been but a curse-
making my body another link
in the breeding chain.
Babies made and born
would determine my worth,
shaping the future, plotting the course.

In another time, not so long ago,
when thoughts of family, love and joy
were reserved for those not like me,
only the daily toil, the unending burdens
anesthetized the senses and dulled the heart
allowing one to survive.

And it is often I'm moved to think
how fortunate it is
that I am NOW, not then-
in that other time, not so long ago.

WILL I ?

Will I be ready
when your time comes?

What about those questions still unanswered,
and the things still undone?

Who will I call for a recipe,
or just to shoot the breeze?

When my melancholy Mondays have me close to tears,
who will make me smile and chase away my fears?

When I'm bursting with happiness
or just have some plain good news,
when I feel like being silly for no explainable reason,
when I want to share a thought, a joke, an emotion--

Where will you be?

Why
will we have to say
"goodbye"?

WITH FLYING COLORS

According to the experts,
I should be a MESS.

If I paid attention to statistics,
I would be
uneducated
belligerent
on drugs
or, in jail.

If they knew what they were talking about,
I would have
babies on both hips
poor odds for longevity
and
some awful social disease.

Because of my DISADVANTAGE,
I should not know
how to deal with men
how to relate to women
or how to bring up children.

But...

when I look in the mirror
and it reflects the person I've become,

I see
someone who is
bright
intelligent
and not too hard to look at.

And
regarding what I've done,
I've gotten married
owned a business
become a professional.

And
on the list of things I have,
I find
friends
colleagues
and many who'd agree
that my single-parent home was
safe
secure
and loving to a fault,

with

a mother who,
even though ALONE,
did
a
fine
job.

ANNE

When she became a mother
our relationship was born.

Once, the little girl
afraid to answer the phone,
now she was the one
with the care of another little girl
in her hands.

The chubby child of long
 ago
who lived in the shadow of
people much too strong,
could finally feel at ease
as her baby looked at her
with trust and dependence.

The teenager of days gone by
who could not blaze the trails
and try new things,
suddenly became the leader, the teacher,
the one with the answers.

When she became a mother,
our relationship was born.

She is my older sister,
she has become my friend.

GOOD TIMES

When times are good,
they're so very very good.

He can make me laugh at the most unfunny things.
There's a link between us that can almost be seen,
a warmth that sears the soul.

When times are good.

My heart turns to jelly as he enters the room.
We giggle through the night as we share
our thoughts
our joys
our fears
our woes.

When times are good.

We plan and plot and chart the course of our lives.
We play and love and love and play,
wrapping one another in a blanket that shields us from
the world.
And we're happy with the knowledge that

When times are good,
they're so very very good.

SUPPOSED TO BE

I was supposed to be a Mommy
last Spring.

I was supposed to be changing disposable diapers
and breast feeding
and rocking him/her for hours in my dark wood,
high-backed chair.

I was supposed to be a Mommy
last Spring.

I was supposed to be planning and hoping
dreaming and loving,
crooning, cuddling,
caring and sharing.

I was supposed to be a Mommy
last Spring.

Then
pain fear
blood and tears.

Supposed to be became...
"We're so sorry Mrs. M".

But,

I was supposed to be a Mommy
last Spring.

ONE OF THESE DAYS

One of these days
you're going to push too hard.

One of these days
I'll stop worrying about what "they'll say".
I'll figure out how to pay the bills
and stand on my own
and be alone.

How I can pack my bags
and not unpack again.

I'll not need the security of
the house
the cars
the fresh-cut lawn.

One of these days
I'll look you in the eye
and say I've had ENOUGH.

And that will be the start of the good ole' days.

One of these days.

LESSON LEARNED ?

I should have known better
than to expect you'd understand.

Although we've been having bad times
for as long as I can remember.

I somehow thought
you'd want to share my joy.

Thought
you'd feel the excitement,
connect with the vibes.

Yes
I know you were asleep.

And
I know you're tired and do work hard.

And
even though you came to the door a little later
wanting to hear the news,

I
now
cannot get past the pain.

The old wounds are open
and

the hurts of yesterday and yesterday
are here again.

I should have known better
that to expect you'd understand.

OLD ENOUGH TO...

I'm old enough to know I should put a coaster under my
glass;
you don't have to remind me.

I'm old enough to know that I should put the cap
back on the toothpaste;
you don't have to tell me.

I'm old enough to know
the steam iron should be emptied after EVERY use,
that dishes SHOULDN'T be left in the sink,
that my clothes should ALWAYS be hung up,
that the LAUNDRY should always be done when the
hamper's full,
that glasses of half-drunk beverages should NOT be
left on the nightstand.

You're old enough to know that my feelings get hurt
when you embarass me in public;
I shouldn't have to tell you that.

You're old enough to know
that a phone call, when you're going to be late, would
be greatly appreciated,
that social engagements should be made jointly,
that differences of opinion DO NOT equal dislike,
that a warm hello, a hug when needed and a touch
WITHOUT SEX are all more than welcome.

Perhaps, one day we'll acknowledge that WE'RE old
enough to know we've both got alot to learn.

NATURAL RESOURCE

I sat this morning and pondered

the right of what we've done

I thought about the road ahead

        and

from whence the strength will come.

The fear is real, the worry great;

will the force soon dissipate?

Or will it be, as days unfold

and we discover how we've fared;

that I can look to left or right

and find my well-spring there?

GIRLFRIEND

When that man asked me, the other day, where he might find my "girlfriend", the little hairs stood up on the back of my neck. You know what I'm talking about---those fine, tiny hairs that are at ease most of the time but come to quick attention in the face of an emotional danger sign.

I didn't understand why I resented his question. And then it hit me. It wasn't his tone or even his query. It was his casual use of that word

girlfriend.

Now, ladies, you tell me...

When you come upon that special female friend and she greets you with "hey girlfriend", there's no doubt in your mind she's happy to see you.

When your phone rings and she says "have I got something to tell you, GIRLFRIEND" don't you just drop whatever you were doing 'cause you KNOW you're about to hear some juicy news?

When that scoundrel you refer to as your man has broken your heart for the 999th time, how do you spell relief? G-I-R-L-F-R-I-E-N-D.

When you are down to your last dollar and the light company the phone company AND the landlord are all camped out at your door, to whom do you turn?

To God and country? Not me! I turn to God and, that's
right,
>   my GIRLFRIEND

So--the next time that man asks me ever so casually,
where he might find my "girlfriend" here's what I'm
gonna' do:

I'm gonna' rear back my shoulders, shift all my weight
to one side, roll my eyes, suck my teeth and say

>   "How dare you take THAT name in vain!!!"

WHAT'S IN A NUMBER ?

You just ought to be ashamed of yourself.
You know you don't have any business
asking me for my friend's number.

I know she looks good and
sparks
all those man-feelings and thoughts
of what it would be like to
wrap her in your arms and
fall in love
again.

How nice it would be to meet
for
that quick drink
and play toesies under the table.

And yes
a quiet interlude in a spot reserved for two
is probably
just what the doctor ordered.

And since I never say never
it's quite possible that she might be ready for a fling.

But
just remember
the next time she passes down the hall
and
your tongue loses its muscle tone,
somewhere
someone
is looking at
your wife.

SAY YOU...SAYS ME

You became his wife
to give me a good life

YOU SAY

I've been nothin' but trouble
and it's burst your bubble

YOU SAY

You coulda' done this, you coulda' done that
without the burden of me on your back

YOU SAY

I'm dumb and lazy
I drive you crazy

YOU SAY

My life will be no good; on that you'll bet,
but what the hell; best take what I can get

YOU SAY

But , guess what...
After years of hearing all the above,
of being made to feel so unloved,
I now know
You ain't so much either.

A LETTER TO MY FRIEND

Some people use the nightly news
as a barometer for the condition of the world.

Indeed, when thinking about where WE are,
it is easy to fall into the trap of wondering
how bad can things really get?
or
has all the good been exhausted?
and does anyone care at all?

But,

in times like these
when personal setbacks have knocked me off my feet,
I look at my own insignificant corner of the world
and I see
caring
loving
and an outpouring of warmth.
There is concern, compassion, unselfishness and
strength.

And
I take heart because I know
this cannot be the exception-it must be the norm.

Though the phrase has been coined
and probably overused,
I see the world as a better place
because of folk like you.

And now,

When I get down on my knees at night
to speak with the Power that is,
I don't ask for
health
wealth
or happiness
until first I've acknowledged how
blessed I am.

Why?

Because of you.

RITE OF PASSAGE

The family hovered-somber in their grief,
warmed and strengthened by the gathering fold.
Few in number, at first,
then
aunt uncle
brother sister
friend and neighbor.

The voices rose in nervous chatter;
the tension built 'til the beams
bent
under the strain.

Then, the
SONG;
the powerful, joyful, tearful
SONG.

The uplifted voices sending their
pain
anger
their hopelessness;
pleading with
HIM
to deliver, in peace
the flesh of their flesh;
singing and praying that the
suffering is ended and the journey
just begun.

LET FREEDOM RING

MY COUNTRY 'TIS OF THEE
Lady can you spare some change?
I haven't eaten in two days.

SWEET LAND OF LIBERTY
I left my legs over in the Nam
right beside my best friend.

OF THEE I SING
Mister, just a quarter--
a dime, a dime will do.
I've got a wife and four small kids,
the baby's got the flu.

LAND WHERE MY FATHERS DIED
I used to have a farm;
grew red ripe tomatoes

LAND OF THE PILGRIMS' PRIDE
and golden, sun-kissed corn.

FROM EVERY MOUNTAINSIDE
Bulletin: an unidentified man was found dead this
        morning in a downtown storefront doorway.
            The apparent cause of death?
            overexposure to underliving

LET FREEDOM RING!

JUST SAY NO

I heard in school today
that when I'm faced with the drug problem
I should

JUST SAY NO.

When the pusher on the corner
offers me a job
so I can get those new shoes I want
or that gold chain I saw
I should

JUST SAY NO.

As I think about it,
those words do make sense.
They've always been a part of my life.

One day my dad looked
at the seven mouths he couldn't feed,
at the bills he couldn't pay,
and told my mom he had to go.
She begged him to hold on--
she knew things would get better.

HE JUST SAID NO.

When my mom tried to find
some low-cost day care for the kids,
so she could go to work-
every place she went

THEY JUST SAID NO.

Then 'uncle' Joe came to live
to help make ends meet.
He took a real liking to my little sister.
Every day, when he took her into the back room,
we heard her crying as she

JUST SAID NO

We call the landlord, daily,
to let him know he should add another room
for the roaches and the rats.
Isn't there something you can do?
We ask.
And he

JUST SAYS NO.

I graduate from high school this year,
and thought I'd be going to college.
I made the grade,
they say I can.
But the financial aid package
was another

JUST SAY NO

All my life
I've been hearing these words.
Now,
as my mouth closes over blue steel,
now,   its my turn to

JUST SAY NOOOOOOOOOOOOOOOOOOOOOOOOOO.

WHAT PRICE EXCELLENCE ?

The future is our children;
they will, they must compete.
There's nothing we won't do, we say,
the standards we've set to meet.

A commitment to excellence,
that's what we've vowed we'll make;
in order to equip our young,
no step's too big to take.

Every innovative tool
that comes to light, we use.
But, in our zeal to trim the cost,
let's not our goals confuse.

IF I COULD PAINT

If I could paint,
what a picture I would create
of what I saw today.

If I could paint,
the canvas would begin stark white--
a nothing waiting to be born.
The nothing would slowly creep away
as a trickle of burnt orange slipped in.
Suddenly, a bold flash of emerald green would appear,
then candy-apple red and sweet plum.
Strokes of sunshine yellow and fawn beige would take
their places.

I would step back from what I'd done.
And thru' the cold winter ahead
I'd simply look at my canvas
and
have my autumm day to warm me.

If I could paint.

COPING

Why look at me, when you talk about
greens cooked in pork?
You assume that
I
must be able to identify.

There was a time when my
anger
was so great and thinly veiled
that I would have harbored
dark thoughts
about you and your
assumptions
and the
boxes
into which your
generalities
could have placed me when, in fact,
my boxes
have nothing to do with you or the
baggage
which you bring to your daily encounters.

Then there was a time in my development
when I would have simply
flashed
one of my "let me smile cause she'd never understand"
looks
at you and waited
patiently
for you to realize a subject change was in order.

THE POEM

I don't know where poems are written,
but I know where they are born--

the robin chirps
leaves change
the baby smiles, a man cries
laughter
loving
the whistling wind
a glance, touch
or
kiss.

I don't know where poems are written,
but I know where they are born.

THE GIFT

Just at that moment
when NIGHT was on the run
skipping away with
LIGHT
licking at his heels,
just at that moment
I
became.

OH YEAH ? OH YEAH!

REFLECTIONS ON...

LUPUS: ROUND ONE

You thought you had me beaten and that I would simply surrender to the abuse you have inflicted on my body and that I'd accomplish nothing more with my life and I'd sit here feeling sorry for myself, bemoaning what I might have done had you not taken up residence.

But, the joke is really on you because in attacking my brain you have triggered some of the best writing I have ever done - it just won't stop - the thoughts and feelings and emotions keep pouring out no matter how much I keep telling myself I can't possibly be doing this because I'm sick.

LOVE GONE BAD

Love gone bad
is like
a refrigerator
that
once
was stocked to the brim
with all kinds of
goody goods
good for you
tasty bites
of
umm-umm
that just kept you
coming back for more
and more
new tastes and
refills
until you realized
that
you'd
forgotten about
the service contract
and
came home one day
to find the box
full
of tiny, slushy-hard
unidentifiable
stuff
for which you no longer had
an appetite.

FAMILY TREE

I used to think it must be nice
to have a family tree.

I envied the German, Irish, and Italian kids
in my class who brought in pictures of their
great great great great greats.

I resented my grandfathers' mamas' refusal
to talk about having been a slave;
I felt she had cheated me out of my
HERITAGE.

She didn't cheat me of a thing.
Whether she knew it, or not,
she was leaving the greatest
legacy
she could.

I did not BEGIN
in modern day slave America.
I was BORN in a paradise of the earths' core.
The roots of my tree are kings and queens;
the branches are warriors, poets and scientists who
don't need names - they simply
WERE.

LISTEN HERE

You think you're going to take my man,
to make him leave my side.
You feel you know just what he needs,
that, in you, he will confide.

He's been bedazzled, you are so sure;
enraptured by your charm,
inside your warm, protective clasp
he's safe from any harm.

With candlelit dinners you woo my man
and dress so hot, so fine.
But, after all that we've been through,
I KNOW the man is mine.

But, there is something I must ask,
at night when lights are dim.
It's a question you have brought to life,
Do I, in fact, want HIM?

I CANNOT TELL A LIE

The moment I did it
I had second thoughts.

Even as I savored every second
I couldn't help feeling
just a bit guilty.

It goes without saying
I wondered what your reaction
would be.
Will he be hurt?
I asked.
Is he going to rage
with fury?

Of course, I then rationalized.
He'd have done the same thing
if the opportunity
had been his;
I've never known him to pass up
a good thing.

There was no question
you'd find out;
we're much too close
to hide something like this
for long.

There's just no way
around it.

When you ask,
and you certainly will,
I'll simply have to
look you straight in the eye
and say
YES,

I

ate the last hot dog.

PERFECT FIT

I heard you today
when you thought there was nobody around.

I heard you as your voice
trembled just a bit.

Mommy
Mom
Mother
Mama
Ma
Moms

I heard you today
trying on your new name.

PURE MAGIC

There is nothing sweeter
than a baby's kiss,
those tender lips, without exception,
turn a grown-up's face to bliss.

The trust which is so evident
when an infant reaches up,
would melt the heart of anyone
no matter how hard, how tough.

When a baby gurgles
and twists and turns and coos,
it's like a magic fairy wand
has chased away the blues.

And when that small one smiles at you
as by the crib you pass,
you're bathed in a euphoria
you hope will always last.

NOT GOODBYE

I want to believe,
I really do,
one day I'll again
be seeing you.

The loss of you
has wrenched my soul;
for you were the part
which made me whole.

They say don't cry,
don't shed a tear;
it's not the end
I shouldn't fear.

One day if I follow
a straight, good line,
I'll hear you whisper
"it's now your time".

IT'S UNDERSTOOD

I trust you.

I
trust
you
enough
to
know
you
know

I trust you.

THE DECISION

What will I think,
              when the sun comes up?

I wonder if your bronze-brown skin
will look as smooth and soft
as it now does.

Will the little hairs on the back of my neck
get all fuzzy and electric
because the muscles rippled in your arm?

I wonder if the low, low bass
of your voice
will light the fire burning inside me, at this instant.

And that twinkle in your eye -
who can say
that it will make me giddy and carefree again?

I guess I'll take the chance
that having to stand on tiptoe
to whisper in your ear
will make me feel safe and secure
              when the sun comes up.

Enough speculation;
what the hell!
It's only midnight - the night's still young.

Deep breath,
quick mirror check.

Hi,
my name is...

HMM...

Isn't it ironic
that you don't think
I
can make a decision?

You say
it takes a clear head
an analytical mind
and a calm, measured process
to reach the right answer,
to make the best choice.

Well
my response is
I
chose
you.

CASE IN POINT

Make note of how he treats her,
that first woman in his life.
You'll find there is no difference
in the way he'll treat his wife.

Does he listen carefully,
when she a word imparts;
and hold her close emotionally
in his heart of hearts?

Are his words soft-spoken,
his temper always even;
or do you find when times get tough
it's he who does the leavin'?

Take heed of what I'm saying,
because it's always true.
The way he treats his mother is
the same way he'll treat you.

46

DO YOU GET IT ?

If I have to explain,
you wouldn't understand.

When I come across the person
for whom no explanation is required,
I'll grab hold and pull him close
and close my eyes
and pray and hope
that I don't wake up
from my
dream.

I KNOW ... YOU KNOW

I feel a headache coming on.

I feel a headache coming on
everytime you

run your right hand through your hair
starting at the tip of your forehead;
ending at the top of your shirt collar,

then shift your two hundred forty pounds
form one foot to the other
as though it were a ton,

then look at the laces on your shoes
as if you'd discovered
a new form of life,

and clear your throat

and proceed to

lie.

CLYDE

I came here several years ago
I was one of seven puppies.
I knew I'd found the perfect spot
in the home of these two yuppies.

When it's time, they let me out,
I whine and I am fed.
And when, at last, the day is done
there's a nice warm cozy bed.

No time for boredom
in this big house
hey - what did they do
with my stuffed mouse?

Playtime's over
enough of that;
I roll over on my back
... I get a pat.

I go to the groomer
every six weeks;
and when I come out
I'm so, so sleek.

Whoever said it's a dog's life
clearly did not know me;
'cause if he had, then you could bet
it's a dog he'd want to be.

THE WAY IT BEEZ

Why don't you react
and tell them how you feel?

It has to affect you
when they treat you
like a child.

The pain pulsates
on your face
every time you call them
mister
and you don't have a name.

And who are they,
these old boy boys
to tell you
your performance is lacking -

when it's purely chance
that they are who they are;
fate it is
which has put them in a position
of having the
luxury
of not realizing
you are

a man.

ONE PLUS ONE IS ONE

Motherhood may never come
but a woman, I know I am.
Even without a baby
I still fulfill the man.

The reproduction of himself
is not his only aim;
he married me for me, he says,
not to play the breeding game.

My womb may never bear the fruit
his seed may never grow,
but down life's road together
he and I will go.

AFTER THE BEEP

Telephone answering machines are a great source of enter-
tainment. It's a wonder it took them so long to be invented.
It's even more curious that many people still resist dealing
with them.

As long as you don't make toll calls, you can't find any
cheaper amusement.

Come on, you say, I've got to be kidding. Let me give you an
example.

I dialed a number yesterday. The voice that answered didn't
even say "hello". Instead, I was greeted with "you have
reached 222-2222". Give me a break! Why, and for whom,
was this machine confirming its own number? If I had dialed
the wrong digits what was I supposed to do now? I guess I
could have apologized for disturbing them, her, it. No - I
would probably have done what I do when I get a human
being on a wrong number; just hang up and hoped the
machine wasn't equipped with caller I.D.'.

What? You still don't believe answering machines can
provide a good laugh? O.K., O.K., here's another one...

What about those folks whose recorded messages begin with
"hello" "hello" hello", leaving you feeling like the fool of
the century because you're sitting there shouting back "hello"
"hello" "hello" while banging on your receiver because
you're sure your equipment must be malfunctioning.I really
like those types. The"friends" who do that to you have
simply found the cure for life's stressful days. It's cheaper
than therapy.

And, oh yes, if you're seriously in need of a good time then...

call someone whose got the latest hi-tech model capable of delivering a greeting which is so long that, by the time it is finished and the musical tone sounds, you haven't got an inkling of recollection about why you called in the first place.

One of my favorites is the machine which challenges the caller to solve a riddle. I must remember to ask that person whether I won a prize when I called last week.

Is that a chuckle I hear? But still not a believer!

This one will do it...

I'll give you a number you can punch in where the machine has definitely missed a beat. It's June, right? Well, this product of the Space Age will perform one of the best renditions of 'Have Yourself a Merry Little Christmas' that you have ever heard.

There is, however, one answering machine experience that I could live without...

Waiting patiently through someone's message only to have the phone disconnect after the tone, because the tape's run out - that's no fun.

I guess that's why I'm glad you invested in the extra long running spool. Please return my call...

when you get a chance.

ON LIFE'S OBSERVATIONS

Do you see those three old ladies?
They're neighbors of my mother.
On living they've got alot of views
they share with one another.

It's their opinion, a collective one,
that life is a true blessing;
with many a puzzle and a riddle
to keep one always guessing.

On the topic of the block's bad child
they stand together, side-by-side,
the mother should find a sturdy switch
and decisively tan his hide.

Those three old ladies really feel
modern medicine's for the birds,
just give them some herbs and roots and such
they'll cure you - mark my words.

Clothing styles come and go, they say.
Yes, to that they can attest.
With what's in the trunks in their three homes
they could pass any fashion test.

They have a proven theory
regarding headache pain.
It's clearly a sure indication
that you've overtaxed your brain.

On the year's first day a man must be
the first to grace your door.
'Cause if he's not, the ladies say,
bad luck's yours ever more.

So if you've got a problem
and see no resolution,
pay a visit to these dear old women;
they'll give you a solution.

IT'S ALL UNDER CONTROL

I told my seventy-one year old mother
to call me
just as soon as her search was over;

that I'd wait, anxiously, by the phone
wishing there was some way
I could help her find

that roll of quarters
which she's sure she hid
last month
so no robbers would find it
even if they were smart enough

to look in the freezer.

PORTRAIT OF YOU

It took me by suprise
when you asked me
if I'd ever wished
I could relive my life.

It made me weep
when you said
that if you could
you'd erase what there's been of
YOU
and then draw your own picture.

IT'S CRYSTAL CLEAR

What would happen to this world
if the women were in charge?
Would the issues facing us
be as frightening or as large?

Women are much too frail, they say
too timid and too weak,
but this earth might be a nicer place
if men were a bit more meek.

Emotion, it's true, just might be
a woman's driving force
but that, plus strength, you must agree
has kept most men on course.

And if all the women of the world
got together and agreed,
then from the threat of war and strife
we'd forever more be freed.

SHEER WONDER

Do you sometimes wonder
about the importance of what you do -
whether your contributions
are simply a drop
in a bucket so large
that your drop seems to disappear before impact,
especially when you hold yourself up
against someone great
who makes one splash after another?

I don't.
Don't get me wrong -
there was a time when I would have said
"I identify".

But then I decided
that while the big splashes
do make a lot of noise
and get everyone's attention,
it's the little drops
that
one by one
replenish the sea of life.

IT'S AN AGE THANG...

You can say what you want,
but 'Do-Wop' is still my thing.
"I Want To Sex You Up" you say?
"Ooh Baby Baby" made my bells ring.

I know, I know, I'm out of step
with the music of today.
But you don't have anybody
who can touch Marvin Gaye.

Your tunes are 'def',
the words are 'slammin'.
The Spinners & the O'Jays,
now they were jammin.

It was the music of the Dells
that I fell in love to.
Could you say the same
about 2 Live Crew?

Aretha demanded "Respect",
refused to be a 'link in the chain'.
And, as for Gladys, huh!,
she was out catching that 'Midnight Train'.

Smokey was crooning,
breaking hearts left & right.
While the Chi-Lites were the sedative
each and every night.

I could go on forever,
but I suspect you'd still call it jive
No matter, no matter,
Mr. D.J. spin another 45.

CASE CLOSED

The sure fire test
of whether a love affair is
over
is realizing
that your best times happen
when
you are apart
and
that
you smile a happy tune
when
you're a solo act.

NO REFUND/NO EXCHANGE

Don't you understand
that the
stuff
you are taking from me
now
is meaning empty?

I will
get another car;
I shall
own another home.

What I will
never recover
is the
me
that I gave
to you
while trying to build the
us
you promised
would be
forever.

BROWN BOY... BLACK MAN
(EBONY DREAM)

I want a brown baby boy
so I can raise a Black Man.
My child man will be the finest
specimen of
understanding
loving
sharing
respecting
giving
caring
intelligence
integrity
sincerity
security
that my love, time & money can buy.

You won't hear my black velvet talking
about needing his space
cause
his space will be so full, so fulfilled.
That ebony male will never
misuse
abuse or
take for granted the women in his life.
He'll find his Black Pearl
and then
he can have a brown baby boy
so he can raise a Black Man.

LOVE'S STORY

YOU

What is it, exactly, you are doing to me?
Before you walked into my space I KNEW who
I
was;
KNEW
what I wanted;
WAS
where I belonged.

Then came
you.
Who are you that you
awaken
feelings, moods, wants
that have lain dormant
for - - ever?

Is it mere curiosity?
I ask.
Or
the temptation of forbidden fruit?
Challenge?
        Impossibility!

What is it, exactly, you are doing to me?
Be safe - stay on the middle road.
No,
there is no midway in me.

I look into your eyes
hoping to see your soul,
searching for the answer

to what it is
you
want
from me.

And
what of my "him" and your "hers"?
I do not do sharing well at all.
I'm still the kid in the sandbox
when it comes to
my friend
my lover
my all.
And yet,
can I ask what I cannot return?

Where is the safety net?
This freefall must end
somewhere.

Who are you?
Are you sure enough in where you are
to guide me through uncharted regions of
me -- of you -- of...?

Understanding there is nothing
casual
in any part of me,
I say
you are the new
us.

ABOUT LOVING

Thank you.
Thank you for showing me that
making love
is not something that happens
in the still of the night
but
something that follows
no time schedule
that
making love
is not the same as
four hands groping in the dark
or
bodies slamming against each other
in a staccato of
gyrations
that
sometimes
climax in a physical release
for one or both parties involved
but is
four hands
lovingly
exploring, touching, sensing
with no start or end
other that the complete
fulfillment
of two people
whose bodies have touched
whose minds have met
whose souls have melted
into one.

Thank you.
Thank you for loving me;
for loving me loving you.

BUTTERSCOTCH BABY

Butterscotch is my favorite flavor.
It's smooth creamy feel
and sweet buttery taste
as it glides on my tongue
cause me to
lick
my lips with sensual delight,
savoring every minute of
pure enjoyment.

Even as the last drop slides
down my throat,
tickling all the way,
I wonder how long it will be
until I can taste it again.

Butterscotch is my favorite flavor,
and
you are
my butterscotch baby.

MISSING YOU

I woke from my dream
             with a smile.

A tear fell when I realized
             you were not there.

WOMAN LOVE

This woman love is something to behold.
Far beyond the physical,
this woman love reaches into the depths
of my being,
touching places only
dreamed of.

That which has been missing is found,
in the tenderness,
the warmth,
the feel
of this woman love.

Wrapped in a blanket of sensuality
blended with the nurturing born
of mother earth
I have found my place
in
this
woman love.

YOU MAKE ME

You make me
  thankful for every new day,
  so glad to be a woman full-grown,
  feel special every time you tell me
   how much I mean to you,
   want to wrap you in my arms
   and never let you go.

You cause me
  to smile merely because I saw your face
  in my mind's eye,
  to take that last look in the mirror
  when I know I'll be seeing you.

Because of you
  my heart skips a beat
  when you walk into the room,
  I hear the birds chirping,
  I see the flowers bloom,
  I feel the warmth of the sun
   again.

Without you
  I would be not whole,
  loneliness would be my companion.
  And, though I would survive,
  the living would not be fun
   because

You make me.
Honey,
you make me.

TEMPORARY INSANITY

Who, who was that person
the one you saw today;
I just could not believe my ears
when I heard what she had to say.

Who, who was that person
with the ranting and the raving;
dwelling on the love now dead
not on the love she could be saving.

The words which poured from her lips
in the heat of the fighting,
were as the wounds of a rabid dog
inflicted in the biting.

She clearly could not stop herself
and lost all self control;
reflecting the anger of the moment
not the feeling in her soul.

You cannot imagine my horror
as the smoke cleared and I could see
that this unrecognizable person
was none other than me.

I'm not asking that you forget today,
but that to me you give
another chance to prove my love;
I'm asking you to forgive.

LOVE SONG

Lying beside you
pretending it's o.k.
as you fall into the sleep
you need so badly
when my
need
is so overwhelming
is akin to
nothing
no one
nowhere
I've ever been before.

You are ever with me;
I smell your smell
touch your touch
even as your spirit
is my sole companion.

I dream you with me
always
and overflow
with anticipation
of making the dream come true.

Yes,
I'll take the
sometime
anytime you are so moved
to give you
to me;

to take me
where only you
can
fly me,
ride me,
send me.

Just bring me
what I cannot bring
myself -
to the place
where there is no name
but yours;
no memory
save the
recollection
of the last time
I journeyed
into
the fantasy of
our reality.

Love me
with the passion
that is
mine for you,
and
I'll tickle taste
your treasure
til
you no longer
beg
me to stop.

SUNSET SAMBA

And they lay.
And they lay
dressed breast bare
on the salt sand carpet
under the sun setting
cotton candy swirls
of end of the day beach fun.

And they lay
in the toast crisp breezes
breath blown on the
froth capped peaks.

And they lay.
And they lay
daze drunk giddy
from
the magic of it all.

THE HONOUR OF YOUR PRESENCE

The honour of your presence
is requested
as this romance
develops
into things
we cannot, as yet,
even
imagine.

APOLOGY ACCEPTED

Love's memory
is only as long
as
the
heart's
most recent
ache.

TRADING PLACES

I know,
now,
how he felt
all those nights
and
mornings
and times
when he reached out
for me
and
there was nothing there

when there was no
magic
he could work to
make me
want him
as he wanted me.

He taught me
what it is to be
desired;
you show me
what it is
to want
and be left
throbbing.

LOVE'S PLEA

Don't
pull me to you
if
you are not ready
to dance
to the
rhapsody you intune
with your
music magic.

COUPON NOT VALID TODAY

Why didn't you tell me
that
after you had addicted me
to a steady intake of
you;
that
just when I thought
there'd be a
never-ending supply
of all that was needed
to keep me alive;
that
just when I got to the point
when
there was no me
without us;
that,
then,
the time would come
when
you'd issue me
a ration book?

A QUESTION OF TIMING

I've sometimes wondered
why
you were not the one
I chose.

I can only muse
perhaps
the choosing
was not mine to do.

At that point in my life
I needed to be
wanted
desired
chased
chosen.

You wanted
a signal light go
and
while you throttled
I got
gotten.

IF YOU...

If you would only
trust
this one last time;
should you be able to
take one more
chance.

I'd simply ask you
to
reach out
your
hand to mine;
I promise
my
hand
won't
be
greasy.

FROM WHERE I SIT...

My Thoughts and Such

FROM WHERE I SIT

And
And the
And the beat And the beat goes
And the beat goes
On
And on
And on
As we
Continue to expend
Our every effort
In the
degradation

    humiliation

       emasculation,

         annihilation
of
US.

MIRROR / RORRIM

Sistagirl
Woman   Friend
Why does my telling you
That
You
Look
Good
Pose a problem for you
For
Us;
Put us in a space
Where
You must question
My motives?

SISTAGIRL
WOMAN   FRIEND
You are my reflection
and
I am yours.

AFEARED NO MORE

I am putting you on
Notice
I am on to you

Yours is not the
Ship of death
On which you
Once
Came for me

      but

I know who you are

The violence
You now inflict on me
Does not fall
As did the
Whip
In the masta's hand

      but

I see you clearly.

Your tongue may not
Spew forth
The Afrikaaner lilt
Or the Mason Dixon Twang

      but

The sound rings forth
With no less biting
Force.

Skinned heads are a poor
Disguise
For once whited-hooded crowns

        and

I see through to the
Core
of your intent.

I am putting you on

NOTICE

I am on to you

        and

as with any malignancy
I will
Now
Pour the limits of my
All
Into a carefully planned
And executed
course
of exorcizing you from my being.

CRACK...SMACK...WHACK...

KILLER   KILLER
Crack kill
KILLER
smack
whack
jack

KILLER   KILL
KILL

birth them
nurse
then
curse them.

KILLER   KILLER
kill
crack smack whack
jack.

Young man old
old
your face but a road map of
Cocaine Alley, Crack Boulevard, Smack Drive;

your eyes - your eyes
the reflection of a
dream deferred.
Deferred?
Lost,
never more to be known.

Young man old
old
old before your time.
What time?
No time!

Can I spare some change?
Change you
to the
YOU
could be
could you have been
before you were
Crack.

KILLER   kill
smack whack jack
You are
crack
smack
whack
jack

BOOM!

EVOLUTION

At the kitchen window she sat
her eyes blood red from
tired,
grandma hands knotted from
toil.

From the kitchen window
oh what she did see,
stirring pots of bad food good;
the world now hers -
the queendom of
tiny ones
watching
older ones
turning
into grown ones
becoming. . .

THE SECRET'S OUT

You've got to be in it to win it
is what they say
about the lottery
of today.

This could be the one,
your lucky day
and you think of the rent
and other bills to pay.

Financial independence could be yours
the ads all scream;
the end of the struggle
realization of the dream.

Take a chance, just one try
don't be a fool;
get that house on the hill
with the indoor swimming pool.

There you go, spend one dollar
to win five million;
never mind the odds
are one in a zillion.

DIAMOND SHATTERED GLASS

Hurt
so bad
deep low
down
hurt
pain
so sharp.

My soul was
open;
my me
exposed.

You called me sister
once;
friend
was my name
for you.

Then you drew
my good memories
sad
and
I will
always
remember you.

AND THEN IT'S GONE

Little woman girl
oh how I wish
I could make you see
that this is
the best of all times.

So ready anxious are you
to feel the feels
and touch the stuff of
big folks
grown folks - old folks who
would give anything
to be able to be
your
little girl
you.

FORTY ACRES LIES & STILL LOOKING FOR THAT MULE

I thought We had reached a point
in our development when
We
could relax, just a bit
and not have to
worry;

thought
some of that
pressure
was relieved and We could
enjoy
life
without constantly
looking over Our shoulders;

felt We no more had to be
better than
to be
just as good as;

figured
the sudden break
in
the still of the night
need no longer
yank us
from Our beds;

hoped the
always
state of fear was but a
memory.

Then I re-learned
that
when it comes to Us
Just Cause
still means
"just because..."

REVELATION

Sittin here waitin
waitin
jump-start ready
waitin for the revolution.

Sittin here watchin
watchin
grafitti-painted fist on mailbox watchin
watchin and waitin
waitin for the revolution.

Sittin here knowin
knowin
I was truly wastin my time
with school-fed lies
knowin and watchin and waitin
waitin for the revolution.

Sittin here livin
livin
from your hand to my mouth
livin and knowin and watchin amd waitin
waitin for the revolution.

Sittin here takin
takin
whatever I can, will, must
takin and livin and knowin and watchin and waitin
waitin for the revolution

Sittin here seein
seein
something happening before my eyes
seein and takin and livin and knowin and watchin and
waitin
waitin for the

WAS THAT THE REVOLUTION ?

LINDA CHOCOLATE SWEET

Chocolate Cocoa
is what your name should be
with those little girl eyes
hiding in the face of
woman
self-assured and confident -
doe eyes
searching
while daring anyone to see
the need you have
to shower your love
but
so afraid to find the
one
with whom you can be
your
Linda Chocolate Sweet
Chocolate Cocoa
self.

REALITY CHECK

I close my eyes
and step
out
of myself
into the endless journey
of those whose sofas
are park benches,
whose cupboards
are garbage cans.

How sad it would be
to have no lock to open
no threshold to cross
at the end of a day
when
the world
has worn me out.

STANDARD PROFILE

Who gave you the right
to
prey on me
to make me fear
for my safety
my security
my well-being?

You are responsible
for
my nightmare studded
sleepless sleeps;

you cause me
to listen for
any interruption
of the early morning stillness
signalling a
breach
in my man-made cloak
of safe and sound.

How has it come to this
that
you are reduced to inhumanity
so raw
that you are memory empty
of what it is to be a
person?

Know this -

know that I will use
every inch of my
humankind
to prevent
my ever
becoming
you.

SELF-ASSESSMENT

The faces of my People
are
ebony
brown beige
butterscotch toffee
and caramel -
shadow hues of
uninvited skeletons
from brutal yesterdays.

The lips of my People
are
happy sad upturns
of back and forth
downs and ups
which bend but never
break.

The eyes of my People
are
pond lily reflections
of soul deep blues
and Bourbon Street
jazz.

But,
in the hearts of my People
lies the
secret to our survival
past
present
and for always.